Mode Dance

Marjorie Seevers

x*ist Publishing

Check out all of the books in the Dancing Through Life Series

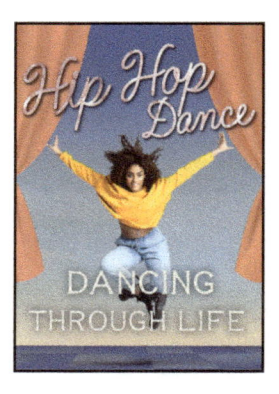

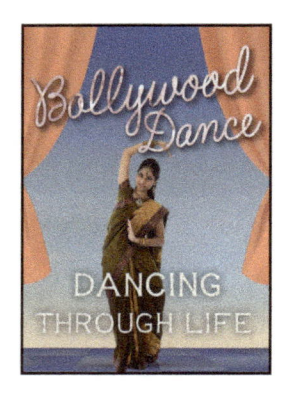

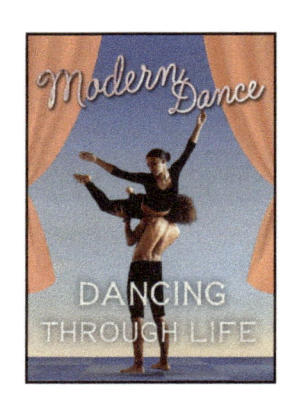

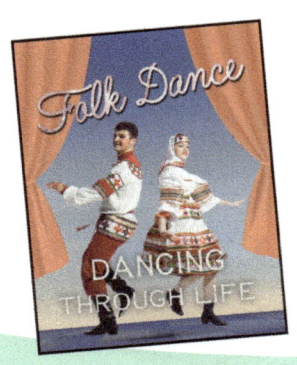

Published in the United States by Xist Publishing
www.xistpublishing.com
© 2025 Copyright Xist Publishing

All rights reserved
No portion of this book may be reproduced without express permission of the publisher.

All images licensed from Adobe Stock

First Edition
Hardcover ISBN: 978-1-5324-5441-7
Paperback ISBN: 978-1-5324-5442-4
eISBN: 978-1-5324-5440-0

Contents

Chapter 1: What is Modern Dance? 6
Chapter 2: Meet the Modern Dancer 10
Chapter 3: Modern Dance Basics 14
Chapter 4: Dressing for Modern Dance 18
Chapter 5: The Big Performance 22
Conclusion 29
Glossary 30
Index 31

DANCING THROUGH LIFE

Chapter 1: What is Modern Dance?

Modern dance is a type of dance that breaks the rules. It is different from ballet and other traditional dances. Modern dance started over 100 years ago. Dancers wanted to move in new and exciting ways. They wanted to express their own feelings and ideas.

Modern dance is all about freedom. Dancers use their whole body to tell a story. They don't always follow a set of steps. Instead, they create new movements. These movements can be big or small, fast or slow. The dancer decides how to move based on the music or the story they want to share. One of the key ideas in modern dance is being yourself. Modern dancers don't try to copy others. They try to find their own style. This makes every dance unique.

Modern dance is also very creative. Dancers often work with different types of music. They might dance to a fast beat or a slow melody. Sometimes, they even dance in silence. The goal is to show emotions and tell a story through movement.

Modern dance has changed a lot over the years. It started as a way to do something different from ballet. Now, it is its own style, with many different ways to move and express feelings. Modern dance is always growing and changing, just like the dancers who perform it.

3

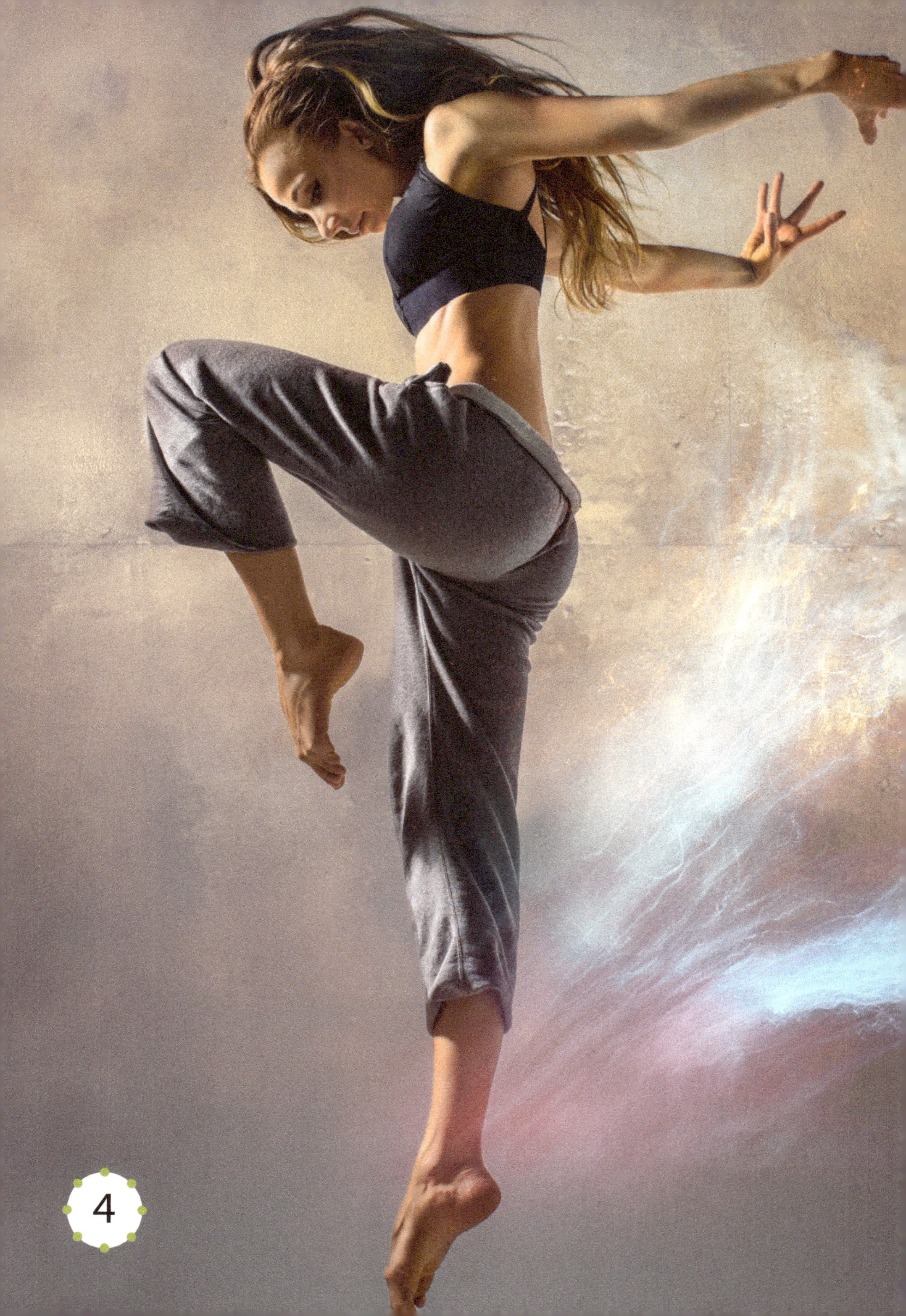

History of Modern Dance: Breaking the Rules

Modern dance began in the early 1900s. During this time, some dancers wanted to do something new. They were tired of the strict rules in ballet. They wanted to move in their own way and express their own ideas. So, they started to break the rules of dance. One of the first modern dancers was Isadora Duncan. She believed that dance should be free and natural. She danced barefoot and wore simple clothes, which was very different from the costumes in ballet. Isadora wanted her dance to be about real feelings, not just pretty steps.

Another important figure in modern dance was Martha Graham. She created a new way of moving called "contraction and release." This was a way to show strong emotions through dance. Martha's dances were often about serious subjects, like love, war, and pain. She believed that dance could tell deep and powerful stories.
As more dancers began to explore modern dance, the style grew and changed. Each dancer brought their own ideas and movements. Some used music, while others danced in silence. Some focused on fast, sharp movements, while others used slow, flowing steps.

Modern dance became popular because it allowed dancers to be creative. They didn't have to follow a set of rules. Instead, they could invent their own. This freedom made modern dance exciting and new.

Today, modern dance is still about breaking the rules. It's about finding new ways to move and express ideas. Modern dancers continue to explore and push the boundaries of what dance can be.

Chapter 2: Meet the Modern Dancer

Who Can Be a Modern Dancer?

Anyone can be a modern dancer! Boys and girls, young and old, can all enjoy modern dance. It doesn't matter where you come from or how old you are. If you love to move and express yourself, you can be a modern dancer.
Modern dance is for everyone. Some dancers start when they are young, while others begin later in life. You don't need special skills to start. All you need is a passion for dance and a willingness to learn. With practice, anyone can improve and enjoy modern dance.

Modern dancers come in all shapes and sizes. Each dancer brings their own unique style and energy to the dance. Some dancers are graceful and flowing, while others are strong and sharp. In modern dance, everyone's strengths can shine.
There are many different roles in modern dance. Some dancers perform solo, using their movements to tell a personal story. Others dance in groups, moving together to create beautiful patterns. Whether dancing alone or with others, every dancer plays an important role.

Modern dance is not just for professionals. People dance modern at schools, studios, and even at home. It's a great way to express yourself and enjoy movement. Whether on stage or in a classroom, anyone can join in the fun of modern dance.

So, who can be a modern dancer? The answer is simple: anyone who loves to dance! Whether you dream of performing on stage or just want to move to the music, modern dance is for you. All you need is a love for dance and the desire to express yourself.

7

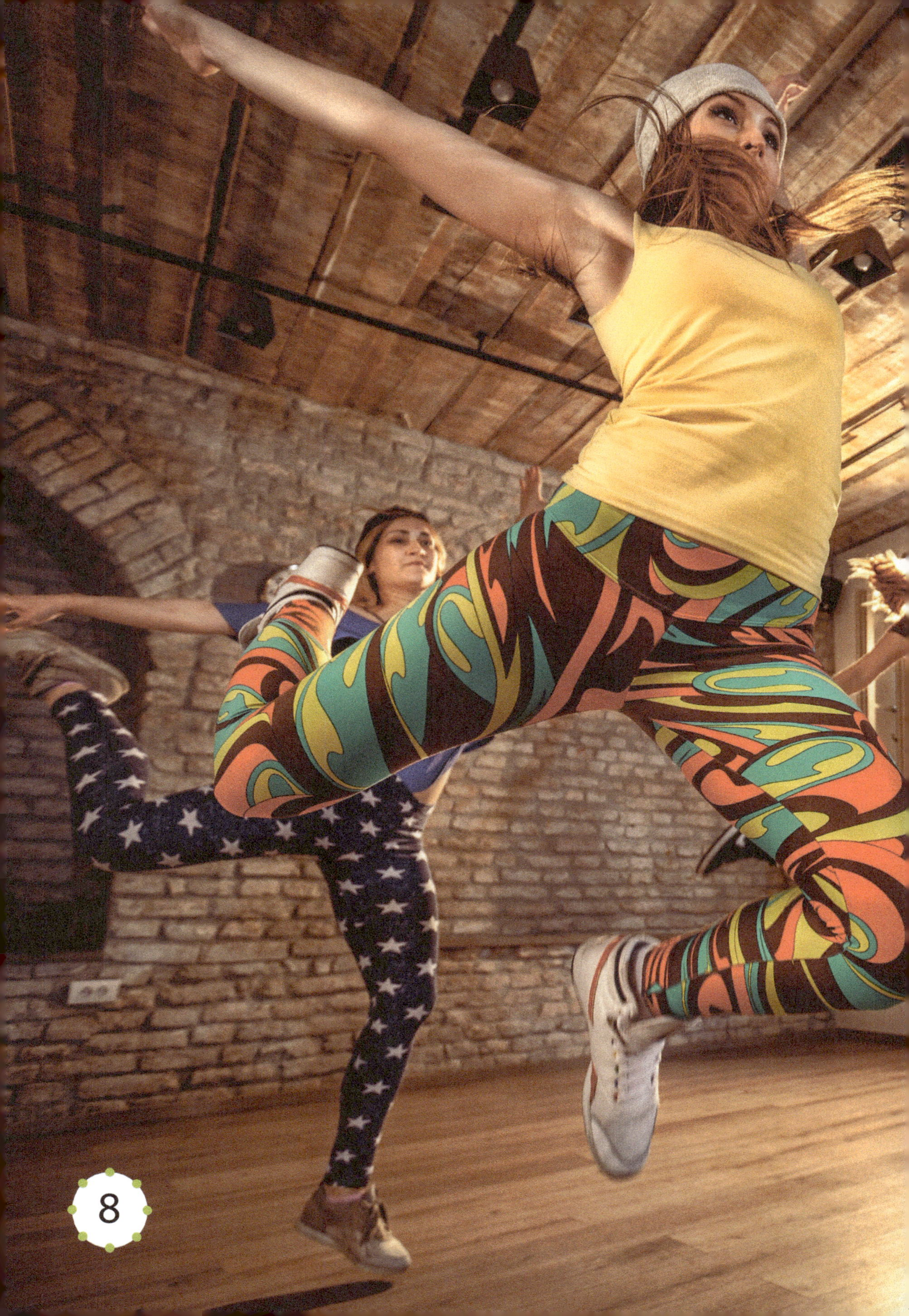

The Different Roles in Modern Dance

IIn modern dance, there are many different roles. Each role adds something special to the performance. Whether dancing alone or in a group, each dancer plays an important part.

One main role is the solo dancer. A solo dancer performs alone on stage. They use their moves to tell a personal story. This role needs a lot of confidence and creativity. The solo dancer is the focus of the audience's attention.
Another key role is the duet. In a duet, two dancers perform together. They might move in sync or in contrast. The duet often shows a bond between the dancers. It could be about friendship, love, or conflict. Working with another dancer requires trust and teamwork.

Group dancers are also important in modern dance. In a group dance, several dancers move together on stage. They create patterns and shapes with their bodies. Group dances can be lively and full of energy. They can also be slow and thoughtful. Each dancer in the group has a role that adds to the overall effect.

Character dancers play a specific role in the story. They might act as a hero, a villain, or a friend. Character dancers use moves and expressions to bring their roles to life. This role adds depth to the dance and helps tell the story.

Improvisation is another role in modern dance. Some dancers create their own moves on the spot. They might respond to the music, the other dancers, or their own feelings. Improvisation is all about being creative and free. It's a chance for dancers to explore new ideas in the moment.

Every role in modern dance is important. Whether you are a solo dancer, part of a duet, or in a group, your moves add to the story. The different roles in modern dance work together to create a powerful performance. Each dancer's style and energy make the dance come alive.

Chapter 3: Modern Dance Basics

Basic Steps and Movements

Modern dance is about freedom and creativity. There are no strict rules, so dancers create their own moves. But there are some basic steps that many modern dancers use.

One common move is the fall and recovery. In this move, a dancer lets their body fall toward the ground. Then, they catch themselves and rise back up. It shows the balance between giving in to gravity and fighting against it.

Another basic move is the contraction and release. In this move, the dancer pulls their body in, like a tight hug. Then they stretch out and open up. This move often shows strong emotions, like fear or excitement.

The spiral is another important movement. In a spiral, the dancer twists their body around, like wrapping themselves up. This move can be done slowly to show tension. It can also be done quickly to show energy.

Floor work is a big part of modern dance too. Unlike in ballet, modern dancers often move on the floor. They might roll, slide, or stretch out on the ground. Floor work lets dancers use all parts of their body in creative ways.

Improvisation is a key part of modern dance. Sometimes, dancers make up their moves as they go. They might respond to the music, the space, or their own feelings. Improvisation lets dancers explore new ideas and find their own style.

These basic steps and movements are the building blocks of modern dance. Dancers can mix and match them to create unique dances. Modern dance is always changing, and these moves help dancers express themselves in new ways.

11

12

Expressing Emotions Through Modern Dance

Modern dance is all about expressing emotions. Dancers use their whole body to show how they feel. The way they move can tell a story without words.

Facial expressions are an important part of modern dance. Dancers use their faces to show emotions like happiness, sadness, or anger. A smile can show joy, while a frown might show worry. The dancer's face helps the audience understand the story.

Body movements also play a big role in showing emotions. Slow, smooth movements can show calm or love. Fast, sharp movements can show excitement or fear. The way a dancer moves their body changes the mood of the dance.

Hand gestures help to add meaning to the dance. Dancers might reach out to show longing or pull in to show shyness. Hands can express what words cannot. They add depth to the story being told.

Posture is another way to express feelings in modern dance. Standing tall with open arms can show confidence. A hunched posture might show sadness or defeat. The way a dancer holds their body can say a lot about what they are feeling.

Improvisation allows dancers to express emotions freely. When dancers improvise, they create moves on the spot. This lets them respond to their feelings in the moment. Improvisation is a way for dancers to explore and share their emotions.

Modern dance is a powerful way to express emotions. Dancers use their faces, bodies, and movements to tell a story. Whether showing joy, fear, or sadness, modern dance helps dancers connect with their audience. It turns feelings into movement, making the dance more meaningful.

Chapter 4: Dressing for Modern Dance

The Modern Dance Outfit: Comfortable and Flexible

In modern dance, the outfit is very important. It needs to be comfortable and flexible. This allows dancers to move freely and express themselves without any restrictions.

Leotards are a common choice for modern dancers. A leotard is a tight-fitting piece of clothing that covers the body. It allows the dancer to move easily and shows the lines of their body. Leotards come in many colors and styles. They are often paired with tights or leggings.

Leggings are another popular choice. They are stretchy pants that fit closely to the legs. Leggings allow dancers to move freely, whether they are stretching, jumping, or rolling on the floor. They are often worn with a leotard or a loose top.

Loose tops are also common in modern dance. These tops are often oversized and flowy. They allow for big, sweeping movements. Dancers might wear a loose top over a leotard or with leggings. The loose fabric adds a sense of freedom to the dance.

Bare feet are typical in modern dance. Dancing without shoes allows dancers to feel the floor. It gives them better control over their movements. Some dancers wear soft shoes, but many prefer the feeling of bare feet.

Modern dance outfits are simple but functional. The focus is on comfort and freedom of movement. This allows dancers to fully express themselves through their dance. The right outfit helps dancers feel confident and ready to perform.

15

16

Accessories and Makeup in Modern Dance

In modern dance, accessories and makeup are used to enhance the performance. They help dancers express their emotions and bring the dance to life. However, modern dance often focuses on simplicity, so accessories and makeup are usually kept minimal.

Headbands and hair ties are common accessories in modern dance. Dancers use them to keep their hair out of their face. This allows the audience to see the dancer's expressions clearly. Headbands can also add a touch of style without being too flashy.

Scarves are sometimes used as props in modern dance. Dancers might hold a scarf and use it to create flowing movements. The scarf can add an extra layer of meaning to the dance. It can also make the movements look more graceful and fluid.

Simple jewelry is sometimes worn in modern dance, but it's usually kept to a minimum. Dancers might wear small earrings or a thin bracelet. The jewelry shouldn't distract from the dance or get in the way of the movements.

Makeup in modern dance is usually natural and subtle. The focus is on highlighting the dancer's features. Dancers often use light foundation, a bit of blush, and natural-looking eye makeup. The goal is to make sure the dancer's expressions are clear and visible to the audience.

In modern dance, less is often more. Accessories and makeup are used to support the dance, not to overpower it. The focus is always on the movements and the emotions that the dancer is expressing. With the right accessories and makeup, dancers can feel confident and ready to perform.

Chapter 5: The Big Performance

Preparing for the Stage

Preparing for a modern dance performance takes a lot of work. Dancers need to be ready both physically and mentally. The preparation starts long before the day of the show.

First, dancers practice their routines many times. They learn every move and step until they can do them perfectly. This practice helps them feel confident and ready. Dancers often rehearse for hours each day to make sure everything looks smooth and polished. Next, dancers prepare their costumes and accessories. Each outfit must fit well and allow for easy movement. Dancers try on their costumes to make sure they feel comfortable. They also check their accessories to ensure they won't get in the way during the performance.

On the day of the show, dancers arrive at the theater early. They need time to warm up their muscles. Warming up is very important to prevent injuries. Dancers stretch and do exercises to get their bodies ready for the performance.

After warming up, dancers put on their costumes and makeup. The makeup is applied carefully to make sure the dancer's face is visible from the stage. Dancers might also style their hair to keep it out of their face during the dance.

Before going on stage, dancers do a final rehearsal. This last practice helps them feel prepared. They go over the most challenging parts of the dance. Then, they take a moment to relax and focus. Dancers might take deep breaths to calm their nerves and get into the right mindset.

When everything is ready, the dancers wait backstage. They listen for their cue to go on stage. Each dancer feels a mix of excitement and nerves. But they are ready to give their best performance.

19

The Joy of Performing Modern Dance

Performing modern dance on stage is a special experience. After all the hard work and practice, it's finally time to shine. The joy of performing comes from sharing the dance with the audience.

When the music starts, dancers feel the excitement. They move with energy and expression, telling a story through their dance. Each step, gesture, and movement is done with care. The dancers feel proud of what they have learned and practiced. As they dance, the audience watches closely. The lights and costumes make the stage feel magical. Dancers connect with the music and with the people watching. They express emotions like happiness, sadness, and excitement through their movements. The joy of dancing comes from this connection.

21

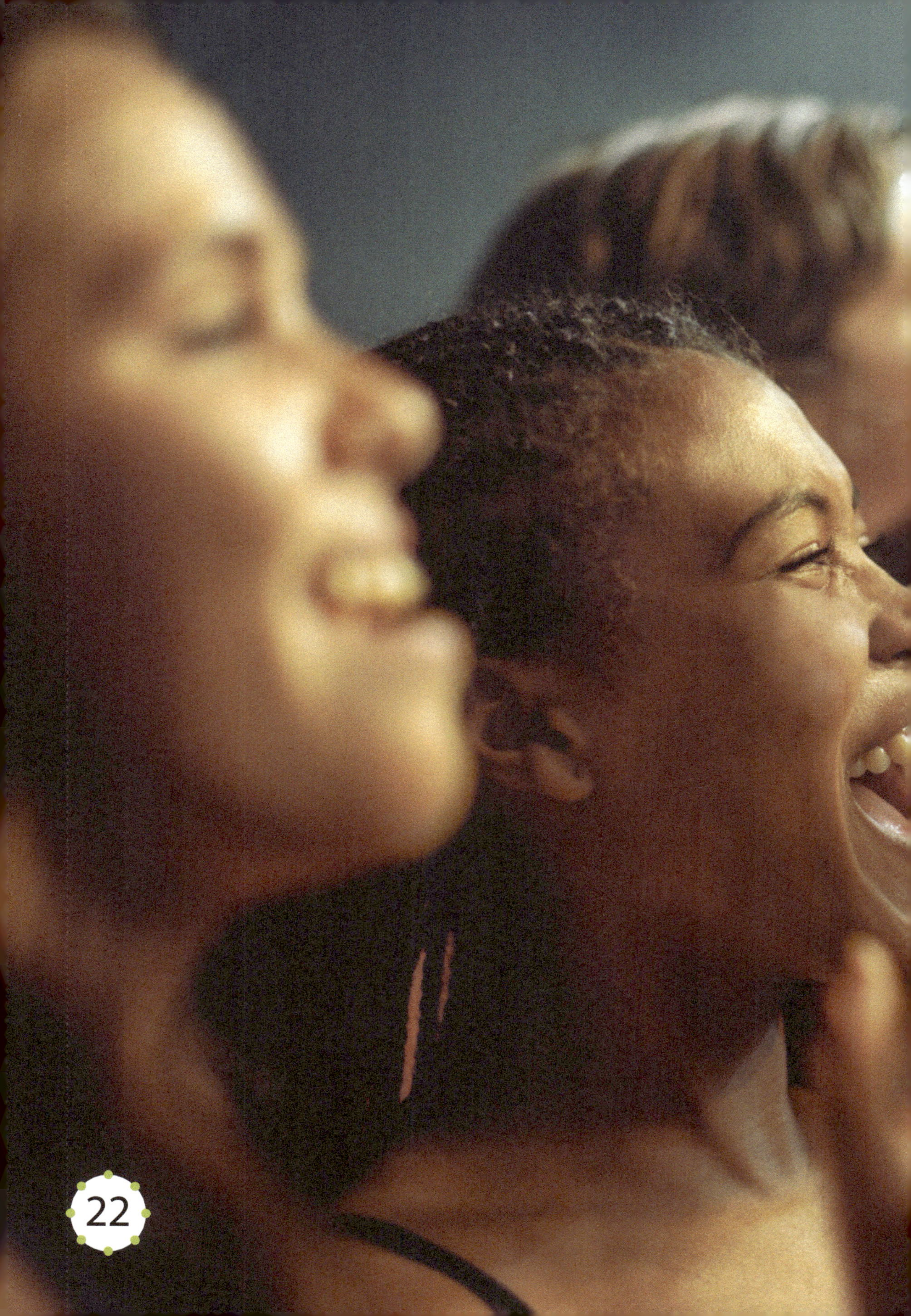

Hearing applause from the audience makes the dancers feel appreciated. Each clap shows that the audience enjoyed the performance. This makes the dancers feel happy and proud. It shows that all their hard work has paid off.

Performing in modern dance can also bring a sense of freedom. Modern dance allows dancers to express their true selves. They don't have to follow strict rules. They can move in a way that feels right to them. This freedom makes performing modern dance even more joyful.

The joy of performing modern dance stays with the dancers even after the show ends. They feel a sense of accomplishment. They know they have done their best and shared something special. This feeling inspires them to keep dancing and exploring new ideas.

For dancers, the stage is a place of happiness and expression. The joy of performing modern dance is something they carry with them in every step they take.

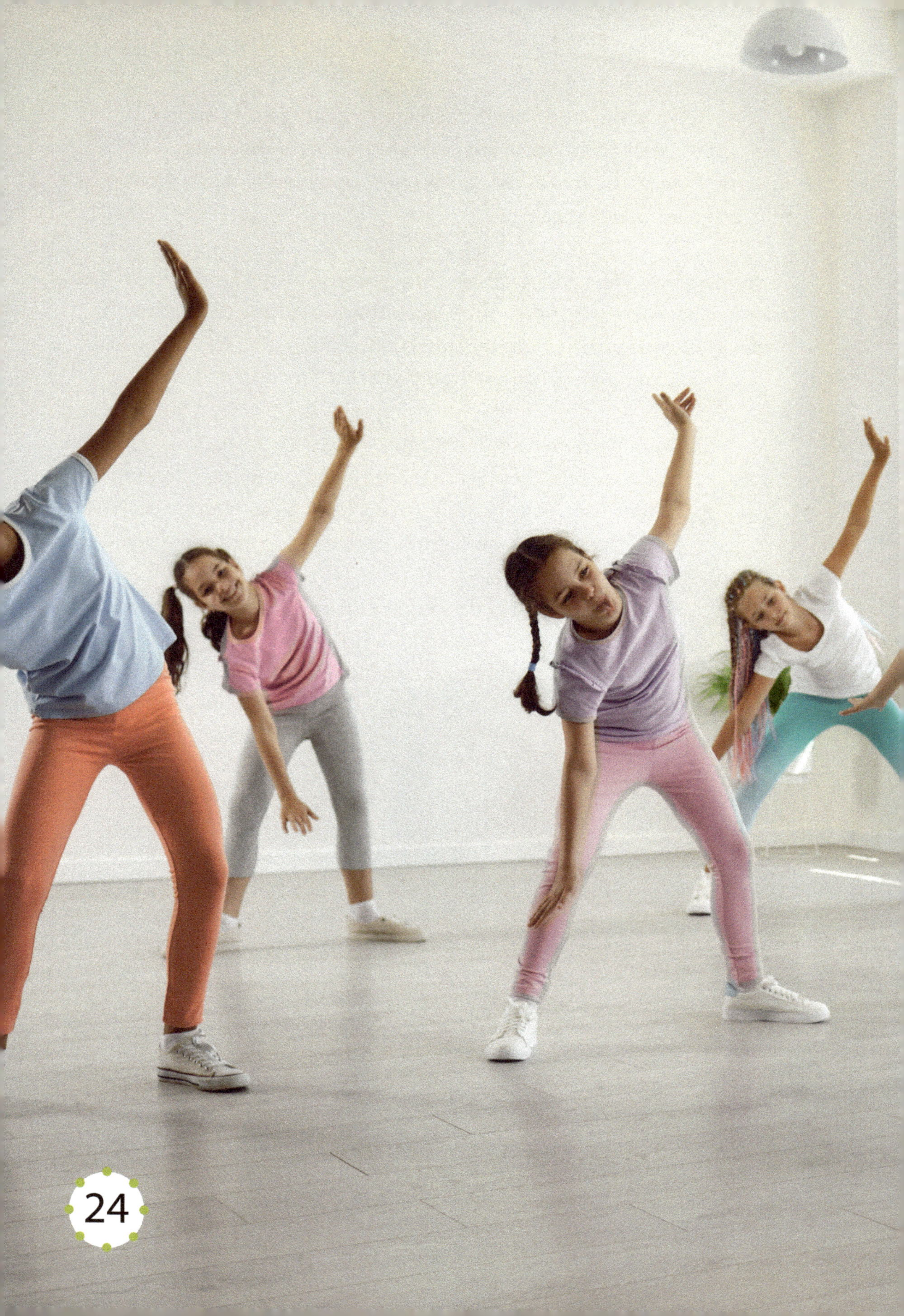

Conclusion

Modern dance is more than just moving to music. It's a way to show feelings, tell stories, and be creative. From learning the basic steps to performing on stage, modern dance teaches us about freedom and joy.

Modern dance lets everyone be themselves. Whether you are just starting or have danced for years, there is always something new to learn. Modern dance is for everyone, no matter your age. It's about enjoying the dance and sharing it with others.

Remember, anyone can be a modern dancer. You just need to love moving and expressing yourself. Whether you dream of performing on stage or just want to dance for fun, modern dance is for you.

Your journey with modern dance is just beginning. There is so much more to explore and create. Whether you are dancing alone or with others, modern dance will always help you connect with your feelings and share them with the world. Keep dancing, keep creating, and let your love for modern dance grow with every step.

Glossary

Contraction	Tightening muscles to create tension in the body.
Duet	A dance performed by two dancers.
Emotion	Feelings expressed through dance movements.
Improvisation	Making up movements on the spot.
Leotard	A tight-fitting dance outfit covering the torso.
Modern Dance	A style of dance focused on freedom and creativity.
Posture	How a dancer holds their body while performing.
Rehearsal	Practice session for a performance.
Solo	A dance performed by one person.
Spiral	A twisting movement in dance.
Stage	The performance area in a theater.
Warm-up	Exercises to prepare the body for dancing.

Index

A
Accessories 17, 18

C
Costumes 5, 18, 20

E
Emotions 2, 5, 10, 13, 17, 20

H
History 5

I
Improvisation 9, 10, 13

P
Performing 6, 20, 23, 25

R
Roles 6, 9

S
Solo 6, 9